DUATHLETE

AENEAS APPIUS

DUATHLETE

A reliable dynamo far beyond
the world of sport

Original edition in German May 2024
Edition in English August 2024

Lecturer: Marcel Nickler
Proofreading: Owen Barron & Chris Griffin
Cartoons: Tamino Appius
Book cover: Aeneas Appius & Owen Barron

Publisher: BoD • Books on Demand GmbH, In de Tarpen 42, 22848 Norderstedt
Print: Libri Plureos GmbH, Friedensallee 273, 22763 Hamburg

ISBN: 978-3-7597-7019-6

TABLE OF CONTENTS

I

ABOUT THE AUTHOR

Success can be planned, learned
and is a matter of the mind.

Aeneas Appius, born in 1960 in Basel, Switzerland, began his sporting career as a football player. At the age of 38, he switched from team athlete to individual athlete and worked his way up to the national top in his age category in running in just a few years. After another achilles tendon operation, his passion for Run-Bike-Run ignited in him. With a great willingness to learn and broad support from the Swiss Duathlon community, he soon challenged the experienced top athletes at international championships.

After 25 years of competitive endurance sport, his achievements include an impressive 280 race victories and over 50 championship medals in different age group categories. He has won international city marathons, bike races, individual time trials, sprint triathlons and can call himself a 3-time Duathlon Sprint World Champion, 4-time Duathlon Sprint & Standard European Champion, 4-time Duathlon Swiss Champion and 7-time Swiss Champion in various running disciplines.

For decades, he analysed the success stories of inspiring people and wrote his first book «WINNING SPIRIT» in 2022. The book reveals the 7 principles of success and teaches the reader how to use the energy of positive thinking as a driving force to achieve big goals.

He is currently involved in the promotion of Run-Bike-Run as Swiss Duathlon Age Group Manager, runs the IG Swiss Duathlon and supports ambitious athletes in achieving their goals and improve competition tactics.

As a management consultant, motivation and performance coach, he supports companies, organizations and individuals in planning and achieving success and thereby spreads the winning spirit.

INTRODUCTION

Live your passion!

The exposé «DUATHLETE» was deliberately written from the perspective of an athlete. It contains the most important characteristics and requirements of an athlete, provides experiences and advice and reveals the fascination of this sport.

Duathlon is a versatile endurance sport combining Run-Bike-Run. All over the world, this popular sport is taught as a physical education subject at school age. The duathlete only needs sport equipment consisting of running clothes, running and cycling shoes as well as a bicycle with helmet. The duathlon is equally popular with children, young people, families, beginners, amateur and competitive athletes and across genders. Young and old athletes can compete in a duathlon competition in different categories. The resulting family atmosphere in this community is very much appreciated by the athletes, sponsors, supporters and spectators.

Run-Bike-Run takes place without external help and without stopping the stopwatch when changing between the individual disciplines. Usually, the duathletes are sent to the first running course from a mass start. The final time is measured at the finish line and separated by different categories and age groups. The intermediate times of the individual disciplines provide the athlete with valuable clues for their race analysis.

The fascination and challenge of duathlon is to complete a mandated route alone and as fast as possible. It is not the best runner or the fastest cyclist who wins, but the one who uses his performance capabilities best and smartest.

Today, a duathlon organizer tries to appeal to as many endurance athletes as possible. A duathlon therefore does not just take place as an individual event. At larger national and international multi-sport events, several sports disciplines such as cycling, triathlon, running and duathlon can be offered conjointly by the organizer. However, the number of duathlon events is significantly more limited compared to cycling races, running events and triathlons. As a result, small national duathlon series with individual and overall series rankings in different age groups are often offered in one season, which brings an additional attractive component for the duathletes.

Worldwide Duathlon events vary in the distances and topologies, which provides a lot of additional and different challenges. Duathlon championships are based on World Triathlon defined standard distances. A Sprint Duathlon is carried out over the short distance of 5km-20km-2.5km, a Standard Duathlon over 10km-40km-5km and a Powerman over 10km-60km-10km. The toughest and longest duathlon competition in the world is currently held annually in Zofingen, Switzerland on the occasion of the Long Distance World Championships over a hilly racecourse of 10km-150km-30km.

Duathlon beginners have already gained initial competition experience in running and/or cycling and are venturing on the new combination challenge of Run-Bike-Run.

The experienced duathlete embodies the essence of a dynamo, always striving to optimise his energy balance. Like a powerful dynamo in the power grid, the duathlete strives to use his energy reserves efficiently, whether by running or bike riding. With great passion and goal-orientation, he devotes himself to his sport, overcomes challenges and achieves impressive milestones. The duathlete's ability to control the flow of energy is reflected in his holistic approach. By continuously optimizing his training, his mental strength and his lifestyle habits, he becomes a stable dynamo that not only drives himself, but also releases a lot of positive energy to those around him. His discipline and goal focus recommend him as a reliable personality as a professional and in private life.

The duathlon as a philosophy of life, the duathlete as a dynamo, a fascinating symbiosis of performance and energy management.

This specialist article attempts to describe and explore what an experienced duathlete is able to achieve and why he loves his sport.

Melanie Maurer, Duathlon double World Champion Elite Long Distance Zofingen, 2022 as well as Middle Distance, Viborg 2022

THE FOUR BASIC ELEMENTS

You can do much more
than you think you can do.

The duathlete is already a (successful) long distance runner and cyclist. He practices long distance running and cycling (road bike, mountain bike and time trial bike) throughout the year and participates in both running and cycling events. He brings his experience from these two sports types to the combination of Run-Bike-Run. In addition to the conventional disciplines, he trains and simulates the multiple changes of sport and his energy management in detail using intensive combined training (sometimes known as brick training). As an all-rounded endurance athlete, he can compete with like-minded people around the world at duathlon events.

The duathlete is a competitive athlete. «I'm going for a run or cyling», is quickly said and done. «I'm completing a duathlon», is a much more complex and larger sporting challenge. Who likes to train different sports and disciplines throughout the year without ever being able to use your skills which you have gained? The duathlete needs a duathlon event with a signposted running and cycling course including a transition area so that he can prove his performance. He can simulate a lot of a competition during the training, but a transition area during a sporting event with many participants is a bit busier and has different dimensions. Depending on the size of the event, a hectic dynamic arises, which demands a much higher level of concentration from the athlete in the transition area than on the competition routes.

The duathlete can be found as an active athlete all year round. As an experienced multi-endurance athlete, he also trains his coordination, mobility, stability, step and cadence as well as muscle and core strength all year round. Depending on where he lives, he complements his winter endurance training with indoor sessions on the bike trainer, the treadmill, the rowing machine and / or enjoys the snow-covered landscape while snow running, cross-country or downhill-skiing. Nowadays, duathlon training and competitions are offered all year round in the virtual world, for example on the Zwift online platform.

The duathlete is an outstanding soloist. He is an always welcomed individual athlete equipped with outstanding skills. He is not training with the purpose to play as a member of a concert ensemble. He earns his recognition with a talented solo performance. As a team member, he may take part in a duathlon relay and/or a team relay competition. Since duathlon is not (yet) an Olympic sport and there is no professional Duathlon league worldwide, the media and sponsor interest is significantly lower compared to Triathlon. The sporting level, on the other hand, is enormously high for both the elite athletes and the age group athletes, despite the less supported financial situation. Since the international trend is towards shorter and more attractive competition formats, every athlete is challenged to further increase their speed, especially when running. The final run of the duathlon makes the solo performance most crucial for the ranking.

Benjamin Choquert, Duathlon World and European Champion Elite
(Photos Fédération Française de Triathlon)

WHAT MAKES A DUATHLETE SPECIAL

The Duathlete runs, cycles and thinks.

As someone driven by vision, the duathlete has a sporting vision. Duathlon is his passion, which he pursues with enormous enthusiasm. Again and again, he feels big feelings of joy. This circumstance gives him a very comfortable feeling of satisfaction. His personal value system defines his morals and guides him through his sporting activities and life.

The duathlete stands out as one of the more unique figures in the vast sports world. He lives his passion for sport which requires a **high level of determination, dedication and self-discipline**. He works on his (iron) will to suffer and his resilience so that he can regularly achieve the goals he has defined in training as well as in competition. Since the human body loves to activate the energy-saving program, he too is required to constantly overcome his own comfort levels.

In a duathlon with a slipstreaming ban (non-drafting) on the bike course, **the duathlete complies with the prescribed distance and overtaking regulations**. Breaking away from a pack of cyclists is not always easy. However, he consciously does not want to gain an illegal advantage and keeps his distance, as he has often practiced in training. Normally one person always notices a violation of the rule.

The duathlete respects the fairness of transition zones. He doesn't want to be hindered and therefore has no intention of disturbing fellow competitors. All athletes are already at an increased stress level when changing disciplines in the transition zone. If a mishap occurs in the transition area, such as accidentally grabbing a neighbor's equipment or throwing down a helmet while running through the narrow corridor of the transition area with many bicycles lined up, it is a matter of honor to correct this slip-up immediately and recover the situation.

Provision of racing bikes and running shoes in the transition aera

Photo Henry Dulink

The duathlete does not seek conscious physical contact with his fellow competitors. If he unintentionally touches someone, he apologises. If he causes a fall, he considers it his duty to offer immediate assistance. **He avoids deliberate disruption and risky manoeuvers that could cause a fall.** The tactic of touching the competitor in order to disrupt his concentration is very frowned upon in duathlon. Experience shows that a person responds to a conscious disturbance with an instinctive counter reaction and tends to release more energy in response.

The duathlete never intentionally slows down an opponent or hinders him when overtaking, whether in running nor cycling. **He refrains from blocking**. In competitions with drafting, several cycling laps are often completed in groups and there is a lot of traffic on the cycling course. Overtaking and lapping situations are increasing. A fast duathlete therefore always checks the safe feasibility of the overtaking manoeuver before a corner or a roundabout and overtakes on the left in right-hand traffic. To ensure that over-taking cyclists can pass easily, a slower biker rides on the side of the road (right or left depending on country), just like in public transport. Once he cuts the corner, the first thing to do is take a quick look behind. Duathlon competition referees monitor fairness and compliance with the rules and may punish unfair manoeuvers with a penalty. It's nice to sit in the penalty box, but time continues to run out and your anger about the mishap is unpleasant.

The duathlete uses technically perfectly functioning material. Since competitions are held in almost every weather condition, he pays great attention to the aspect of safety in order not to endanger himself and others unnecessarily. The range of marginal, even faster and lighter material on the market is constantly growing and tempting. Accordingly, the regulations for the use of equipment in competition also changes regularly. The duathlete avoids a disqualification due to a rule violation by studying the equipment regulations of the Triathlon Federation in detail beforehand. **He does not engage in material doping** and wants to avoid violating the fair play code and or being labeled as a material doping offender. The duathlete understands that it is ultimately the human factor with his aerodynamic position on the bike that offers the optimal balance of cost, benefit, and performance.

The successful mastery of a duathlon with several disciplines and different use of equipment fascinates the duathlete. Since he constantly wants to optimise and improve himself as an athlete, he sets measurable goals and works focused and hard to achieve them. His top priority is to achieve his defined ambitions, regardless of their complexity. To do this, he needs not only a lot of passion, but above all great discipline and the courage to remain self-determined. **The duathlete is a self-determining enforcer.** Every time he achieves a goal, no matter how small, this will further strengthen his self-confidence. This, in turn encourages him to set even more ambitious goals, which can be, for example, participating in a longer competition or a national/international championship.

Parade of Nations at the Duathlon World Championships in Targu Mures, ROM 2022

To be able to run and cycle even faster over different distances, the duathlete specifically develops his endurance strength. This enables him to achieve high linear wattages on the bike for as long as possible, to maintain good body tension and a stable running style on both running sections. **He has a very high endurance power.** His intention in training is not to reach the highest peak values (neuromuscular loads) on a regular basis, but rather to keep his endurance performance just below the anaerobic threshold for as long as possible. He knows that in Run-Bike-Run the final run is extremely demanding and that a sprint on the home straight can still determine the classification. The duathlete therefore intends to experience and enjoy the finish line with enough energy in his body. He doesn't want to miss out on this reward for the weeks of preparation. Duathletes with ambitions for a podium place train alongside endurance strength, especially the ability to sprint with fast, repetitive running units (intervals) on the 400m track. What a duathlete has not stored in his muscles and in his brain, cannot possibly be recalled during competition.

Mastering major physical challenges is not always easy. The duathlete constantly tries to push his physical limits. To succeed in this, he trains his endurance performance on the limit of his anaerobic threshold. If he moves in the anaerobic range for too long, in a state of so-called overpacing, he will pay for it later in the competition with acidified muscles and a drop in performance. The weather can change at very short notice and rain showers, wind or heat change the current situation. The duathlete needs the ability to react flexibly to body signals and rapid environmental changes. **He is an accomplished and experienced crisis manager** and prepares alternative plans in advance with a reduced pace in order to somehow still reach the goal safely. As a good crisis manager, he always carries a small emergency reserve (food, breakdown material, etc.) and knows mental tricks to overcome potential motivation disorders at critical moments. With his experience, he bridges difficult situations with ease and routine, always getting the best out of an unfortunate situation.

Anita Appius focused despite the pouring rain

The duathlon season in Europe usually lasts about six months. During this time, only a few events offer the duathlete the opportunity to achieve his sporting highlights and goals. **The duathlete is an experienced planner.** Training and nutrition planning will help him to be in his best possible shape on the day of the competition. The duathlete plans his trips to the various competition venues, including equipment transport, in a timely and meticulous manner. Since the duathlon season often starts in spring, ambitious athletes like to travel south for training camps or take advantage of the option of altitude training. Only very few experienced duathlon coaches offer valuable and reliable support in training, competition and nutrition planning.

The duathlete studies the competition regulations of an event with sufficient time and creates a schedule from the arrival at the competition venue to the starting gun (horn). In each case, a lot of time passes for the check-in procedure with various start numbers to be attached, equipment checks, positioning the bike and personal equipment in the transition area as well as the route inspection and the warm-up. The duathlete is aware that small mistakes can quickly happen with unpleasant consequences if he must work under too much time pressure in the preparation phase. **He is an excellent time manager**. His time management with a defined countdown (for example 120 minutes) from arrival at the competition location to the starting signal is demanding and is carefully monitored by him. Experienced duathletes recommend planning twice the countdown time needed for a running or cycling event.

The duathlete works on a continuous improvement process and always sets himself new, even more ambitious goals. With his inner drive and enormous endurance, he ambitiously strives to push his limits. **He relentlessly strives for success.** He receives praise and recognition from those around him for his performance. Such positive encouragement increases his motivation and drive to achieve even bigger goals.

To become even faster and more efficient, the duathlete repetitively practices important movements until they become routine and habitual. In the transition zone in particular, his brain is extremely challenged understanding the detail of the situation with the release of the competition adrenaline. To maintain maximum concentration, the fast automatic actions that have been practiced over and over again now help the duathlete to change disciplines very quickly. **He has a high level of automatic ability** to do things without engaging the mind with the necessary low-level details. As a result, he gains valuable seconds in the transition zone, among other things.

Personal performances in duathlon are measured in watts or watts per kilogram (watts/kg), seconds, kilometers or miles per hour (kmh, mph), steps, cadence (rpm) and heart rate (bpm). These are a few reliable performance parameters that the duathlete takes into account. His motto is: **Get faster, with more relaxation!** Many duathletes use different electronic sensors for speed and power measurement, which display and record the desired information when running and cycling. With the support of continuous monitoring, an attempt is made to optimise the speed and performance more and more. In cycling, power profiling as a performance diagnostic tool is used to predict competition performance (maximum values over the time axis) and helps to determine the training intensity to aim for more precisely. Such findings make it possible to carry out most of the training in reduced stress ranges.

The duathlete loves speed optimisation. He assesses his maximum performance on personally selected test tracks for running and cycling. For him, progress means being able to complete the test route faster with a lower heart rate. With a good aerodynamic position when cycling, he tries to keep his drag coefficient extremely low and thereby save some wattage. Special attention is paid to the aerodynamic helmet. This must be suitable for quick putting on and taking off.

Daan de Groot NED, European Champion Elite Middle Distance, Alsdorf 2019

His high level of tactical understanding helps the duathlete to correctly assess and use his own energy reserves at specific points. Since he wants to avoid a drop in performance at all costs, he must behave very cleverly tactically throughout the entire competition and pay attention to the measurement of his data and listen to his feelings, his mind and his inner voice. **He is an experienced tactician** and constantly weighs up whether restraint and patience might be the better option, or to what extent an attack to the finish could give him an advantage. Duathletes know their strengths and weaknesses very well and they build their race tactics accordingly.

The duathlete is a master of flexibility. The reality is that no two races are exactly the same in the world. Each race has different race conditions, rules, course profiles, transition zones and meteorological conditions. Duathlon events with different formats are also offered, such as run-bike, bike-run and cross with mountain bike. To be able to compete in several races in one year, the duathlete needs a very high degree of flexibility. He loves variety and diversity and specializes in short (sprint) or long race distances with competition durations of 1-2 hours or over 3 hours. Short-term changes by the organizer are always possible, for example due to weather or traffic. Therefore, the duathlete takes part in the official race briefing attentively. He remains mentally flexible and can quickly adapt to the new circumstances.

Duathlon is a physically and mentally demanding sport. It requires strong mental resilience. Body and mind must remain in balance for the entire duration of the competition. Right from the start, it's all about being able to master the various disciplines one after the other as hard as possible at the personal limit and without breaking in, while fighting against pain and exhaustion. Mental strength plays a very central role so that what you have trained over and over again can be recalled and implemented at the crucial moment. Completing an endurance competition close to the physical limit demands everything from the mind and body. The duathlete makes the most of his positive mindset. **He matures into a mentally strong hero**. Every negative thought is disruptive and must be able to be transformed into a positive one under stress and pressure. Giving up is not an option for the duathlete, unless he is in danger of physical injury or bad luck with the equipment. Mental training helps him to keep his thoughts in the positive zone and to repeatedly achieve defined goals. The most experienced duathletes can complete a competition in their minds before the real race and see and feel the joy of crossing the finish line. This ability to visualize enables them to be fully focused and to react to unforeseen events during the competition and to implement their own competition tactics more effectively.

Daniel Parpan, Aeneas Appius, Mark Thomson with joint mental activation at the Transilvania Motor Ring, ROM 2019

To find the location of the bike while under stress during the competition in the transition zone, the duathlete memorizes the assigned location and the routes (run-in, bike-out, bike-in, run-out) during preparation. To do this, he runs the routes to and from his changeover position several times and looks for non-removable markings (e.g. flagpoles, light poles, advertising banners, etc.) that helps him to find his position safely in the competition. He learns to divide the competition course into small segments to activate the competition program prepared in his brain selectively with mental hooks if necessary (anchoring). **The duathlete is a master of visualization**. He takes the opportunity to inspect the course before-hand so that potential hazards such as obstacles, tight corners, slippery and narrow sections, U-turns, critical points, course markings and the green and red lines are known. Mental anchors help him to focus on these critical points in time during the competition.

An ultra-fast descent before the red line needs to be practiced.

In his mind, the duathlete is a few steps or cycle wheel revolutions ahead and can recall the many times practiced and mentally stored programs from his subconscious. In his mind, he repeatedly thinks what he should do before and after a specific event, such as the change of disciplines in the correct order. **The duathlete thinks ahead** and doesn't waste any seconds. He remains highly concentrated and starts consciously and with enthusiasm into the next discipline.

The duathlete shows courage. It takes courage to be passionate about multiple sports and disciplines with varying paths and only a few races each year, and to put yourself out there in this way. He cannot hide in the crowd of athletes at a race and is known to present himself as a soloist. As a result, he is noticed, admired and receives encouraging support. This recognition helps him to eliminate any feelings of insecurity more quickly.

The duathlete is constantly testing his limits in terms of safe and fast handling of the equipment under different conditions and performances. **As a competitive athlete, he needs a calculated willingness to take risks** for different terrain, variable weather conditions and to make small personal progress without exceeding the limits of his ability. He doesn't attempt any risky manoeuvers that might end in a fall. If he speculates on a win, he must be mentally prepared to take a higher risk at the appropriate moment.

The duathlete has already earned his spurs as an individual athlete and is now venturing into even more. The duathlon sports literature available on the market is rather modest. As an exotic figure in the big wide world of sports, he appreciates the encounters with the few like-minded people to an even greater extent. The constant dialogue with experienced duathletes becomes an indispensable success factor for him. Before each race, the duathlete studies the conditions and specifications of the competition very seriously. **He is willing to learn and able to engage in dialogue.** It is only thanks to his high willingness to learn, the ability to engage in dialogue and quick comprehension, as well as learning by doing, that he continues to develop.

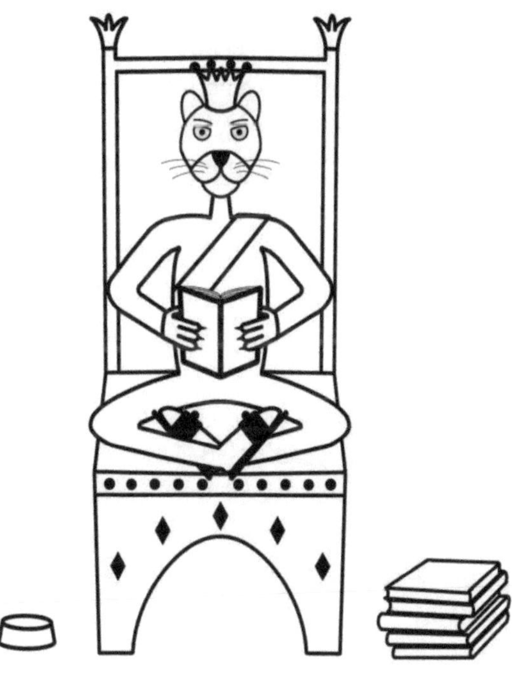

Anyone who trains and maximizes his body's performance inevitably pays attention to a healthy diet. The duathlete regularly checks his body weight and develops a good awareness of sugar consumption. His motto is:

Low sugar - more power!

Every carbohydrate contains energy and enough protein is essential for endurance muscles. How much energy a duathlete needs, to master a duathlon at the planned competition pace, must be found out individually. He thinks deeply about his nutrition before, during and after an event. **The duathlete is a real energy freak.** He thinks about the best nutrition plan for the competition. Beforehand, he practices fluid and food intake of the selected products in competition simulations under high physical performance. He always tries to achieve the optimum and learns very quickly from nutritional mistakes. He prefers this experience in training rather than in racing. He tries to absolutely prevent a drop in energy during a race due to a lack of or incorrect nutrition.

The duathlete is a master of rapid regeneration. As an endurance athlete, he trains in several sports, which increases the time his body is under stress. Only good and rapid regeneration will help him to improve his performance in the medium term. He therefore relies on regular and sufficient sleep and an adequate amount of training that suits his daily work routine. He uses the nutritional pyramid, avoids foods that impair regeneration and is cautious when it comes to alcohol consumption. If necessary, he temporarily supplies his body with any additional nutrients it may need (supplementation).

The duathlete carefully considers which equipment is best suited for use. **He is clever in the selection and use of his equipment.** That's why he inquires in advance about the appropriate requirements for shoes, bike (frame size), pedals, electronic gears, chainring and

cassette, aero handlebars, seating position, braking system, helmet, glasses, clothing and measurement sensors, among other things for a smooth and quick change of sport. It's the details that interest him. He doesn't choose the most delicate high-tech carbon shoe. When making his choice, he checks the possibility of an ultra-quick entry and whether special elastic lacing can be used to avoid tying the shoe. The cycling shoe has a quick-release strap and is clicked into the pedal and fastened in the correct position with a rubber band waiting for the foot to be put in. The strap makes it easy to close and open the shoe while cycling. He trusts and loves his equipment and uses it accordingly consciously and purposefully. A bike fitting is often used for performance-optimised and aerodynamic cycling. He learns quickly from mistakes. He has also learned from third parties that earrings, necklaces and finger rings can lead to unnecessary stressful situations and incidents when taking off a helmet or getting caught on objects during competitions.

The duathlete is one of the most physically and technically accomplished athletes. He competes in several sport disciplines and makes optimal use of the possibilities of his material. **He has a lot of skill and technical understanding.** Especially on the time-trial bike, the duathlete tries to ride in an aerodynamic position at high speed for as long as possible, which requires honed steering skills and high responsiveness. If he is familiar with the equipment, he can recognize weak points and signs of wear in good time and can maintain his training and competition equipment himself. His technical understanding is required when recording a duathlon with the desired performance data from different electronic sensors while running and cycling.

The duathlete quickly learns that he can develop further in his fringe sport primarily through the ability of an open dialogue. **He is a good networker** and maintains regular contact with experienced experts from different fields. In addition to his direct advisors, supporters and sponsors in duathlon, he is looking for other confidants who will help him in his specific development in running and cycling. Many duathletes maintain memberships in several sports clubs. The duathlete treats his partners benevolently and with respect. His personal team is happy to support him and is delighted to be able to truly celebrate successes with him. Experienced duathletes are happy to take on a mentoring role and are mentors to newcomers and rookies. Just as they were able to experience it themselves.

The duathlete loves his data and images. It is not the number of hearts, thumbs up or kudos received on the numerous online platforms and social media or the KOM (King of Mountain) victories that really count for the duathlete. At best, they give him additional wings and bring him joy. Rather, the duathlete loves to meticulously analyse his training and competition data. From the analysis, he derives his optimisation potential. To make this very easy for him to handle, he thinks about which sensor data he needs and where it should be transferred. This is the best way for a flexible evaluation of the performance data and to draw the right conclusions while running and cycling. For example, the development of one's own VO2max value while running and cycling over the years can be interesting. The duathlete memorizes many beautiful and lasting emotions. These positive moments are enormously important to him, as they have a lot of energy potential. In this way, he records the event data, associated images and videos so that they can be quickly retrieved later. He consciously uses the performance data and images for his physical and psychological (mental) development.

Photos Henry Dulink

Only very few people master complex projects successfully because they often cannot muster the courage to implement them. Anyone who dares to take part in a duathlon wants to achieve the project with success, be it as a courageous finisher or as a podium athlete. The duathlete has the experience to successfully lead a project to the finish line. He learns quickly from mistakes and defeats. He knows that there are only a few duathlon competitions available during a season and there is no second attempt. This requires him to work in a very goal-oriented manner to be successful again on the day. **The duathlete has a very strong winning mentality.** The dropout rate of athletes participating in a duathlon in all age groups is lower than 1%. Only those who defeat themselves are strong. The duathlete is a winner type.

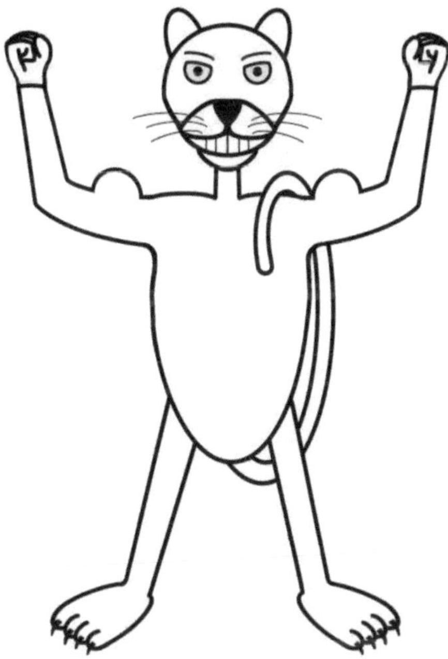

It is an absolute no-go for the duathlete to miss out on the personal award and recognition on the podium as a prize-eligible finisher. Such behavior amounts to a lack of respect towards the organizer and fellow participants. The duathlete always has the stature to show appreciation to the organizer and the competitors with his participation on the prize ceremony. **He is patient and distributes praise and appreciation.** For the duathlete it is a great honor to compete in a competition. He is aware that the many volunteers make it possible for him to have wonderful experiences at events. He is an extremely grateful person and surprises volunteers and sponsors with warmth. He is also pleased with the performance of his fellow competitors and thanks them for their fair play after a race. The current heroes of the duathlon scene are role models for young and old. Being able to benefit from their experience is not a given. For this reason, the duathlete kindly thanks his idols for exchanging experiences.

The welcome greeting is a matter of respect between the teams in team sports. The duathlete, on the other hand, trains specifically and often alone. **He enjoys greeting other athletes**, whether while cycling or running. The duathletes greet each other with a handshake and wish good luck before a competition. This is not only a gesture of mutual respect, but also reminds the athlete of the fair play code.

WHAT ELSE IS SAID ABOUT THE DUATHLETE

When the pain comes,
the duathlete begins to laugh.

The duathlete is a non-swimmer. This statement is courageous. Of course, duathletes also know that swimming is healthy. Experts today confirm that a duathlon with a Run-Bike-Run is mentally and physically more demanding than a triathlon with a swim-bike run. The duathlete uses the non-swim time to improve his ability to run the second run session in a competition at the same speed as the first one. He wants to make sure that he doesn't collapse on the final run after the hard Run-Bike cross sessions. Triathletes have developed a love for swimming. They invest a lot of time in swim training and often forget that their competition ends with a final run and the running time is significantly longer compared to the swimming time.

The duathlete uses short breaks. When running or cycling, there are always situations that cause an ultimate stop. Be it a closed railway crossing, a red light, a parked car, cows on the road and so on. For the duathlete, these are everyday situations when training on open roads. In such moments he maintains inner calm. He stops his training watch, enjoys the brief moment with a rest and some food, relaxes his muscles and takes a deep breath. Because he's about to get back to being fully concentrated.

The duathlete thinks ahead for others on the open road. His rapid speed is underestimated by the public on the open road. To protect himself, he must increasingly think for others and recognize dangers early on. In cycling training, he relies on sections of the route that allow him to ride quickly in an aerodynamic position. He often avoids cycle paths with pedestrians, as the risk of accidents due to inattentive walkers, children and dogs is high. Motorists often show little understanding and are happy to correct people. They often don't notice that they aren't allowed to drive over 30 or 50 kmh in urban areas. Bus and truck drivers rush their 40-ton trucks along the country road, sometimes recklessly, past cyclists. The duathlete learns to be prepared for such situations. This is because the unpleasant gust of wind often hits its aero wheels unfavorably and causes turbulence.

The duathlete signals any danger he notices. He knows the hand signals to indicate danger and applies them in group bike rides and group runs both in training and in competition. He cares about everyone's safety. He signals dangers to other athletes behind him in good time. The late warning of a stone, a hole in the road surface, a threshold, a sharply closing corner, a railway and tram track, a post, a slippery spot, a barrier or a planned overtaking manoeuver can have devastating consequences.

The duathlete prefers the aesthete to the poser. A duathlete's place of work is in nature. He enjoys beauty and as an endurance athlete and aerodynamic architect, he tries to merge with the topology of nature. Optimisation interests him and is his main focus. Unnecessary equipment or weight hinders the duathlete in his intentions. He focuses on his passion and not on the display of his equipment. He motivates those around him with emotional reports of nature, experiences and performance.

The duathlete is a proud member of the community. He moves in a sports bubble with few like-minded people. Since they meet several times a year at a duathlon, they know each other. During a competition you measure yourself as a competitor and afterwards you happily exchange experiences. Each community member gives the others due respect and recognition for their accomplished achievements. This creates a very appreciative, friendly and family atmosphere. Many duathletes also maintain contact on private occasions throughout the year. The best friendships always grow from shared, unique experiences. Duathletes who even compete in international championships represent their country as duathlon ambassadors. The community pays them the greatest respect and honors them appropriately.

International community impression (IRE, LUX, SLO, GER, SUI) at Duathlon European Championships Targu Mures, ROM 2019

THANKSGIVING

Gratitude is the secret of happiness.
(Dalai Lama)

I am fortunate to be able to thank many people who have tirelessly supported and motivated me in writing, designing and translating this book in several languages. I would particularly like to mention:

my beloved wife Anita Appius for her immense support and patience, my friend Marcel Nickler for his appreciated editing work, my Swiss duathlon friends Stefan Marty, Mark Thomson & Reini Pöllinger for their content ideas and review of the script, my Irish duathlon friend Owen Barron as well as my English duathlon friend Chris Griffin for the English translation assistance and my son Tamino Appius for the drawing of the panther cartoons.

Subsequent patrons have financially supported the publication of this book with generous donations. Thank you very much!

- ALTIUS Swiss Sportmed Center
- Appius Consulting
- Crespo.ch GmbH
- Interest Group (IG) Swiss Duathlon
- Powerman Zofingen, Duathlon World Championships

Benjamin Choquert, Duathlon World Champion Elite Pontevedra, ESP 2019 (Photo Fédération Française de Triathlon)

With his diverse abilities, the duathlete is developing into a valuable and reliable dynamo in our society.

www.duathlet.com

LONG DISTANCE DUATHLON
POWER MAN
SWITZERLAND
WORLD CHAMPIONSHIPS 
Nº 1 IN RUN – BIKE - RUN
www.powerman.swiss